flip through this **book**

and **do** something

totally

random!

by T. Bugbird

Designed by Annie Simpson
and Charlotte Stratford

with thanks to the students of Bridgewater School
and Mia Hazell Liyanage

random

RANDOM
LIST NO. 1

What's the most random . . .

1. meal you've ever eaten?

....

2. hairstyle you've ever seen?

....

3. shoes you've ever worn?

....

10. thing you've ever worn
    in your hair?

....

11. present you've ever given?

....

....

12. present you've ever received?

....

mmmmm!!

Snack ATTACK

Make a CARTWHEEL sandwich!

1 Take a slice of fresh bread and trim off the crusts to make it square.

2 Use a rolling pin to roll the bread lightly so it's about 1/4 in (5 mm) thick.

3 Spread a thin layer of jelly.

4 Carefully roll up the bread. Secure the roll with a few toothpicks.

5 Put the roll in the fridge for 10 minutes to help it stick together.

6 Take the roll out of the fridge, remove the sticks and carefully cut 1/2-in (1-cm) slices.

Instead of jelly, why not try cream cheese or ham?

My all-time TOP 10 SNAX

1
2
3
4
5
6
7
8
9
10

Delicious and totally spiral!

Which flavor ice cream are you?

What's the scoop on your ice-cream personality?

- Become a vet
- Become an actor

- Sport
- Dancing

- Write romances
- Write mysteries

- Day
- **start here**
- Night

- Sandcastles
- Snowballs

- Doodles
- Crosswords

Cookies & Cream
Super-sweet: you treasure your friends and have a creative mind!

Sleepover

Surprise party

Strawberry
Full of energy and positivity: you love challenges and making people happy!

Scrapbook

Secret diary

Neapolitan
Complex personality: you are full of surprises and nobody knows what you'll do next!

Team sports

Drama club

Coffee
Sophisticated and thoughtful: do people know the real you?

random

Transform these doodles into works of art by

doodles 1

adding arms, legs, faces, or anything you want!

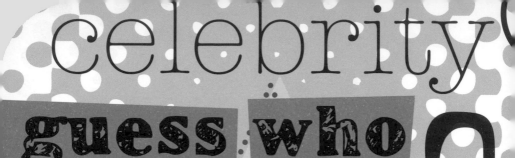

celebrity

guess who?

You may think you know your favorite celebs but can you spot them without seeing the whole picture? Take the **celebrity guess who** challenge and find out!

1 Get together with some friends and a stack of old magazines. Cut out pictures of your favorite stars, making them roughly the size of the purple box on the next page. Don't let the others see your pics!

2 Get your friends to look away, and then put a picture in the purple box (use a little piece of tape to hold it down) and cover it with a small piece of paper, about the size of the box.

3 Slowly lower the paper one space at a time. The first person to guess the name of the celeb wins the number of points on the left side of the box.

4 If you want to play bottom-to-top, use the scores on the right side of the box. Keep playing until someone reaches 100! **Celeb-a-licious!**

**Start
at the
top**

0

50

20

10

5

3

2

1

1

2

3

5

10

20

50

or **Start
at the
bottom**

O! mix it up

Creating party-mix lists of your favorite songs is a totally cool way to fill random moments.

Think of the five songs that best suit the mood, moment, or person!

5 songs for my
crush

....
....
....
....
....

5 songs for my
best friend

....
....
....
....
....

5 songs for a
party

. . . .

. . . .

. . . .

. . . .

. . . .

5 songs for my
best teacher

. . . .

. . . .

. . . .

. . . .

. . . .

5 songs for when I
feel sad

. . . .

. . . .

. . . .

. . . .

. . . .

5 songs for when I
feel happy

. . . .

. . . .

. . . .

. . . .

. . . .

Random Sandwich maker

**Craving a sandwich?
Not sure what to have?
Do you dare to eat what
the random sandwich
maker is serving up?**

1 Decide how hungry you are on a scale of 1 to 10 (1 = not hungry, 10 = starving).

2 Add this number to your age.

3 Let's say your answer is 16. Work your way through the fridge from left to right, starting at the top shelf. When you get to 16, cross off the item – that's your first ingredient! Keep counting in 16s, jumping over any box that has been crossed, until you get to an item on another shelf. Keep going until you have an ingredient from the third shelf.

Cool combo or disgusting dinner?

Cheese
Sausage
Chicken
Beef
Egg
Tuna
Meatballs
Salmon
Shrimp
Fish sticks

Tomato
Cucumber
Carrot
Beets
Grapes
Pickled onions
Pepper
Celery
Apple
Onion

Mayonnaise
Ketchup
Jelly
Pickle
Brown sauce
Coleslaw
Bar-B-Q sauce
Mustard
Horseradish
Salt and pepper

Random!Random!Random!

hair&
make-up
studio

Give the models party-perfect hair.

Curl it, straighten it, or add extensions and cool colors.

random puzzles

would you rather...

join a band **or** join a circus?

live in a tree house **or** live in a cave?

dye your hair bright pink **or** paint your fingernails jet black?

hold a slug **or** tickle a fish?

dive in a pool of custard **or** jump in a bath of jello?

lose your phone **or** break your MP3?

dance with your friends **or** dance with your crush?

Stare at the icons for one minute, and then turn the book over and see how many you can remember.

How are you feeling?

Find as many words as you can to describe how you might feel today.

E	M	B	A	R	R	A	S	S	E	D	A
A	A	S	V	E	X	C	I	T	E	D	O
T	D	E	S	I	R	U	B	R	A	V	E
S	E	D	O	R	D	W	L	E	Y	T	N
B	O	T	I	R	E	D	R	S	O	C	V
Y	H	A	P	P	Y	T	I	S	N	U	I
L	B	U	W	A	D	K	N	E	D	E	O
R	T	O	O	B	O	R	E	D	Z	X	U
S	E	L	I	V	M	G	O	O	D	I	S

1. _____
2. _____
3. _____
4. _____
5. _____

6. _____
7. _____
8. _____
9. _____
10. _____

It's totally delicious, but ...

do you know how CHOCOLATE is made?

Chocolate starts as **beans**, growing in pods, on the trunk of the **cacao** or **cocoa tree**. The beans come out of their pods covered in liquid. They are put in huge piles to drain and to develop their flavor. Next the beans are dried to develop their taste further. Then their shells are removed to reveal **"nibs,"** which are roasted and ground into a liquid, or **"liquor."**

When it cools, the liquid becomes solid. This solid **"mass"** is pressed to make cocoa butter, which is used to create **chocolate**. What's left becomes **cocoa powder**, which is used in beverages or for cooking.

Delicious chocolate was enjoyed by Aztec tribes in South America over 500 years ago!

To produce chocolate, the **"mass"** is combined with milk and sugar to make **"chocolate crumb." Cocoa butter** and **"liquor"** are added to the crumb to make **chocolate**. A thick mix is used to make bars, while a thinner mix is used for chocolate coatings.

There are three main types of chocolate: **dark, milk,** and **white**. Dark chocolate has high levels of cocoa, which makes it dark, while milk chocolate contains milk, making it a lighter color. Some people say white chocolate isn't really chocolate at all because it doesn't contain any chocolate liquor (just cocoa butter) – which is also why it is white!

THINK YOU KNOW YOUR CHOCOLATE?
HOLD A CHOCOLATE TASTE TEST!

Take 5 of your favorite chocolate bars and break them into bite-sized pieces. Blindfold your friends, give them a piece of chocolate to taste, and see if they can name it.

Award 1 point for each bar correctly identified. Whoever scores the highest gets to keep the chocolate!

Up until 100 years ago, chocolate was a luxury drink enjoyed by the superrich. Then new methods of producing solid chocolate were discovered, which made it cheaper and available to everyone.

random

Transform these doodles into works of art by

keep

trade

Look at the list below, and then decide what you'd keep, what you'd swap for something else, and what you'd throw away!

1   Swimsuit   Platforms   Poncho

2   Adam Lambert CD   Chris Allen CD   PCD CD

3   Cell phone   MP3 player   TV

4   Leopard-print purse   Shutter shades   Waffle maker

5   Harry Potter novel   Signed photo of Corbin Bleu   Hair straighteners

6   Jonus Brothers CD   Red jelly shoes   Black nail polish

7   Banana   Orange   Pineapple

or trash?

8 Magazines: *Tiger Beat* American Cheerleader Teen Vogue

9 Smoothie Maker *HSM* DVD Gold gladiator sandals

10 Britney CD Photo of David Henrie Year's supply of potato chips

11 Tutu Tiara Barrette

12 Ashlee Simpson CD Paris Hilton CD Rhianna CD

13 Box of chocolate Box of peanuts Box of popcorn

14 Tickets for: Katy Perry Kelly Clarkson Pink

15 Bagel Hot dog Waffle

16 Jeans: Guess Von Dutch Lucky

Find the 8 random objects hidden in the flowers!

Rearrange their first letters to spell a tasty snack!

movie madness

HOLLYWOOD
PRODUCTION _____
DIRECTOR _____
CAMERA _____
DATE   SCENE   TAKE

Who would play you in the big-budget movie of your life? Who would play your best friend? Who would play your mom? Now's the time to find out!

CHARACTER LIST

CHARACTER LIST

1 Write the names of 8 friends or members of your family in one of the CHARACTER LISTS. Give each a random number from 1 to 8.

2 Write the names of 8 celebs in the cast wheel.

3 Next figure out what number day of the week it is. So here's what you do if it's Saturday: Saturday is day 7, so begin at the star at the top of the wheel and then count seven places. Where you land is your starting point.

4 Take the number you gave each character and work around the wheel clockwise from your starting point, until you land on the celeb who will be playing the role. Great casting or totally RANDOM?

CAST WHEEL

Top tip!
Use a pencil so you can erase and start again!

draw in 3D

Drawing in 3D is really easy and looks AMAZING!

Here are some basic shapes ...

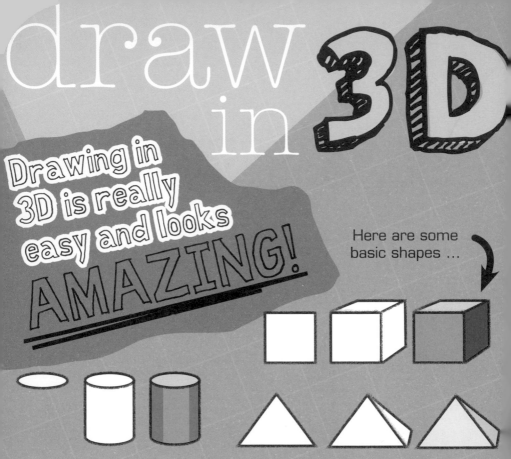

See how **color** makes the effect **stronger**.

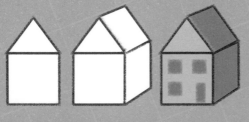

Any shape can become 3D – this **square** and **triangle** have just become a **house!**

3D letters and numbers make a great graffiti style.

A B C D E F G H I
J K L M N O P Q R
S T U V W X Y Z

1 2 3 4 5 6 7 8 9 0

And **3D bubble writing** makes delicious doodles!

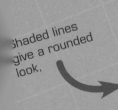
Shaded lines give a rounded look.

Hello

How Tall?

Which stars are the same height? Draw a line to match the stars on the left with celebs of the same height on the right.

Mariah Carey 5 ft 9 in (1.75 m)

Taylor Lautner 5 ft 10 in (1.78 m)

Robert Pattinson 6 ft 1 in (1.85 m)

Venus Williams

Simon Cowell

Tyra Banks

would you rather...?

Look at this picture. Do you see a beautiful vase, or two girls looking at each other?

change your name **or**

change your age?

take a rocket to the moon **or**

swim to the bottom of the ocean

have x-ray vision **or**

fly like a bird?

write a hit song **or**

star in a movie?

be famous and poor **or**

unknown and ric

HEADLINE NEWS!

Newsflash! These hot headlines are missing two VITAL ingredients – the names! Write the name of a rock star, actor, or anybody famous in one of the boxes, and then write the name of one of your friends, family members, teachers or anyone you know in the other. Can you handle the scandal?

to perform duet with

is secretly crushing on

to star in movie with

seen in restaurant with

to be paid $1m to star with

 Q Who was the first woman in space **?**

A Valentina Vladimirovna from Russia, in 1963.

what does your *writi*

Some people believe that your handwriting can reveal your true personality.

WHAT DO YOU THINK?

big handwriting

REVEALS AN OUTGOING PERSONALITY. THIS PERSON COULD BE A LOT OF FUN!

small and neat

People with small, neat handwriting are more likely to be quiet and thoughtful. They may not be the life of the party but they'll make a true BFF!

Upright handwriting

Upright handwriting is a sign that the writer is independent. A strong personality like this can make a lifelong friend!

Slanting forwards

Slanting forward suggests the writer is a good communicator – this person will always let you know where you stand!

slanting backwards

Slanting backwards suggests the writer is a private person. They may not be the easiest person to get to know but the effort will be worth it!

swirly and curly

Rounded letters with lots of curls and loops indicate an imaginative, creative personality, while narrow, less loopy writing can indicate a dependable and businesslike personality!

ng reveal about you

Ask your friends to write their names here.
What does their handwriting tell you?
Do they agree?

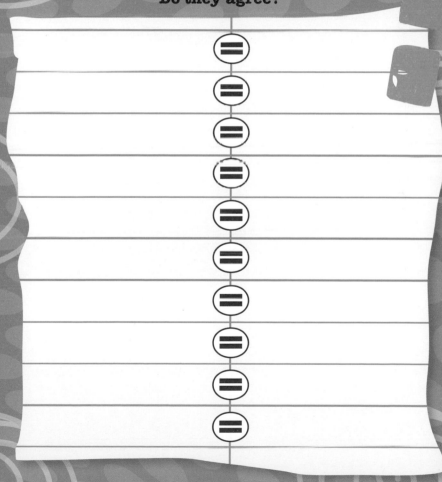

random snack facts

POTATO CHIPS were invented by a New York chef, George Crum, in 1853. George was annoyed by a customer who kept returning his fried potatoes because they were too thick and soggy. To get him back, he cut the potatoes into thin slices and fried them so they were crisp and impossible to pick up with a fork. But his trick backfired – the customer loved them!

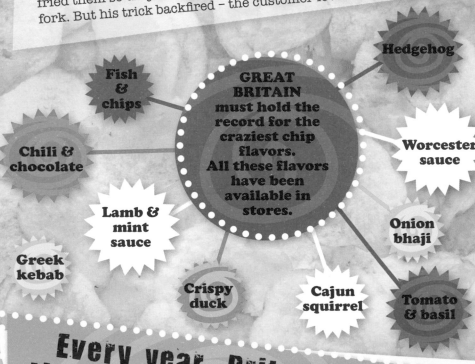

GREAT BRITAIN must hold the record for the craziest chip flavors. All these flavors have been available in stores.

Hedgehog

Fish & chips

Worcester sauce

Chili & chocolate

Lamb & mint sauce

Onion bhaji

Greek kebab

Crispy duck

Cajun squirrel

Tomato & basil

Every year, Britons chomp through over 9 BILLION bags of nuts and snacks.

One of the most popular snacks in the world is the soft **PRETZEL**. People have been picking at pretzels for more than 2,000 years! The biggest pretzel in the world was baked in Louisiana – it was over (3 m) wide. **12 feet**

Nobody likes a snack like a New Yorker! The city has more than 4,000 street-corner snack vendors.

That's nothing compared to the world's longest hot dog. That was made in Tokyo in 2007 and measured over 200 ft (63 m) long!

Cheese, please!

Germany

Netherlands

Italy

France

Around **18 MILLION** tons of cheese are produced in the world every year.* The top cheese-producing nations are:

United States

* According to The Food & Agricultural Association of the United Nations in 2004.

9 random things to do on a boring car

1. Randomize your name

Rearrange the letters of your name – or anybody else's – to make a name that's totally random.

So Chace Crawford could become Ache C. Drofwarc, and Selena Gomez could become Leenas Zogem!

2. practice your signature!

3. Try to remember how many different hairstyles you've had in your entire life.

4. A–Z Game

Think of a subject, then take turns thinking of words starting with each letter of the alphabet (so if the subject was boys' names, the first could be Aaron, the second Brendon, and so on). If you can't think of a word, you're out of the game. The last player left wins.

tripiration

485

5. Try counting backwards from 1,000 without falling asleep . . .

890

126 **234**

6. Celebrity guess who

Think of a celebrity then get everyone to take turns asking a question about "you" until your identity is revealed!

7. make a list of 10 things you'd like to do or achieve over the next year.

8. Don't tell the truth!

This game is harder than it sounds. Ask 5 easy questions, for example, "What day is it?" or "How old are you?" The person answering must give an incorrect answer. If they pause or tell the truth, they are out!

9. Try to remember everyone in your favorite class, in the order in which they sit.

twisted WORD

Eleven of these names are hidden in the word search. They are linked together like a crossword puzzle and have one thing in common. Once you've figured out what it is, finding all twelve will be as easy as counting **1 2 3!**

Ava	Sarah
Rachel	Jennifer
Shannon	Briony
Josephine	Mariah
Monique	Isobel
Sam	Samantha
Jacqueline	Destiny
Lucy	Hayley
Katie	Cassandra
Charlotte	Keisha
Mackenzie	Angelina
Olivia	Vanessa
Sophia	Veronica
Alexis	Jenny
Mollie	Louise

SEARCH

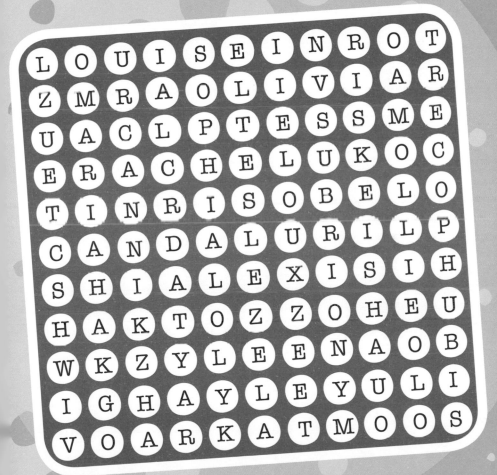

RANDOM
LIST NO.2

What's the most random …

1. homework you've ever been given?

....

2. text message you've ever received?

....

3. book you've ever read?

....

10. thing you've ever worn to a party?

....

11. earrings you've ever seen?

....

12. day out you've had with your family?

....

4. thing you've ever had for breakfast?
....

5. thing you've ever traveled in?
....

6. hair color you've ever seen?
....

7. ringtone you've ever heard?
....

8. show you've ever seen?
....

9. color you've ever painted your toenails?
....

13. hat you've ever worn?
....

14. hat your mom's ever worn?
....

15. color you've ever wanted to paint your room?
....

designer

Celebrities simply cannot have too many designer bags. Design your own collection!

doodle bags

Add handles to the bags, or bags to the handles.
Add buckles, straps, and pockets, and then give your bags
a personal twist using your favorite patterns and colors.

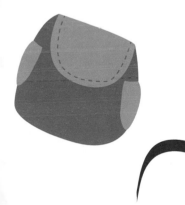

What's yours called?

Sometimes bags are named after the celebrity, place, or object that reminds the designer of the bag.

For example, one of the most famous bags is the Fendi Baguette (pronounced bag-et), which was named after a baguette – a long French loaf of bread!

FISHY!

Which of these isn't a fish?

Angelfish

Catfish   Dragonfish

Spoonfish   Clownfish

Glassfish

These celebrity names have been totally randomized. Sort them out, then match them up!

Mariah	stew
Lady	ododwrenu
Justin	darceffil
Kelly	ibereb
Britney	nella
Jordin	ekalmitber
Kanye	agga
Miley	twifs
Justin	pearss
Kevin	skraps
Lily	sanjo
Carrie	sucry
Selena	slonrack
Taylor	repry
Daniel	reyca
Katy	zemgo

Fill in the missing letters to reveal **three** famous faces!

_ANES_A H__GE_S

AYLO __UTN_R

RO_E_T _AT_IN_O_

99 kitten names!

Scratch	Ginger	Paws	Boss	Prince	Taylor	Charles	Tab	Buttons
Ozzy	Pepper	Smoky	Radar	Echo	Jupiter	Sox	Lazer	Marbles
Ripley	Fuzz	Deisel	Duke	Tibbs	Butch	Bones	Frisbee	Jet
Foxy	Dash	Puddles	Nugget	Dash	Stripe	Egypt	Puss	Snowy
Earl	Tom	Sebastian	Harry	Jaffa	Pogo	Tom	Walnut	Nano
Bamboo	Felix	Bop	Taco	Sheeba	Nana	Lily	Kiss	Honey
Precious	Sugar	Flora	Sequin	Minnie	Jewel	Diva	Venus	Jessy
Tabitha	Gucci	Bubble	Dusty	Princess	Missy	Bliss	Kisses	Opal
Sadie	Kitty	Cara	Classy	Sapphire	Star	Martha	Ellie	Gracie
Cuddles	Sunshine	Queen	Sassi	Candy	Diamond	Biffle	Mama	Curly
Cookie	Berry	Violet	Sparkle	Cherry	Mitzy	Penelope	Agnes	Tessa

celebrity

who would you choose to ...

give you fashion advice?

....

teach you to dance?

....

help you with your homework?

....

share a room with?

....

go on vacation with?

....

go to a party with?

....

give you a makeover?

....

teach you to sing?

....

cele

bff

teach you to drive?
....

go shopping with?
....

redecorate your room?
....

run a marathon with?
....

cohost a TV show with?
....

restyle your hair?
....

cook you a meal?
....

drive you to school?
....

brity

keep ♥ trade

Look at the list below, and then decide what you'd keep, what you'd swap for something else, and what you'd throw away!

1   Fake nails   Fake lashes   Hair extensions

2   Taylor Swift CD   Leona Lewis CD   Lily Allen CD

3   Peanut butter sandwich   Bag of pretzels   Bag of nachos

4   Waffle maker   Juicer   Toaster

5   Photo of: Taylor Lautner   Robert Pattinson   Zac Efron

6   20 Snickers bars   Signed poster of Channing Tatum   Spongebob DVD

7   Ham sandwich   Cream cheese bagel   Potato wedges

or **trash?**

8 Autographs: Gwen Stefani   Jay Z   Jordin Sparks

9 Jo Bro T-Shirt   5 Britney CDs   200 Markers

10 Hair scrunchie   Beanie hat   Cowboy hat

11 Novels: Romance   Mystery   Adventure

12 Biker boots   Running shoes   Ballet pumps

13 Tickets for: American Idol   Dancing with the Stars   The Phantom of the Opera

14 Beanbag   Armchair   Deckchair

15 Mobile   DS   CD Player

16 Suite Life DVD   Twilight DVD   Fame DVD

design
your own
logo

Your logo should be unique to you, and it should say something about the kind of person you are. So think carefully about the shapes, colors, and any words or pictures you use.

For example, if you use lots of pink, and heart shapes, your logo will tell everyone you are romantic, while a star shape tells the world you are born to be famous!

You can use your name, nickname, or just initials. Remember to keep it simple so you can draw your logo again and again!

Here are some ideas ...

You see logos everywhere! They're on magazines, storefronts, clothing, and even everyday appliances. Having your own logo is totally cool. You can draw it on your notebooks, make logo badges, or even make a sign to go on your door.

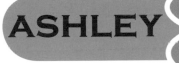

ASHLEY

ashley

A

AND THE WINNER IS . . .

Hold your own awards ceremony!

Put some glamour into your day by holding your own celebrity awards! Think of three nominations for each category – then survey your friends and family, count the votes, and host a special sleepover or party to announce the winners.

Favorite TV show   **Votes**

1 ....

2 ....

3 ....

Favorite author   **Votes**

1 ....

2 ....

3 ....

Favorite TV actor   **Votes**

1 ....

2 ....

3 ....

Favorite TV actress   **Votes**

1 ....

2 ....

3 ....

Favorite music group   Votes

1 ....
2 ....
3 ....

Favorite music artist   Votes

1 ....
2 ....
3 ....

Favorite movie   Votes

1 ....
2 ....
3 ....

Favorite movie actor   Votes

1 ....
2 ....
3 ....

Favorite movie actress   Votes

1 ....
2 ....
3 ....

All-time hero   Votes

1 ....
2 ....
3 ....

HOLLYWOOD
PRODUCTION
DIRECTOR
CAMERA
DATE   SCENE   TAKE

invent a
smoothie

Blitz your favorite fruit
with some ice, apple juice,
and plain yogurt for the
best smoothie ever!

Pear
ORANGE
BANANA Blackberry
Apple Cherry
Raspberry
Kiwi Fruit
APRICOT
Watermelon Peach
Grape Redcurrant
MANGO
Blueberry Melon
STRAWBERRY
Pineapple

Each time you try a new combination,
write it down, and give your recipe a
taste-test score out of 10.

```
........................................
........................................
........................................
........................................
........................................
   ——
   10
```

```
........................................
........................................
........................................
........................................
........................................
   ——
   10
```

```
........................................
........................................
........................................
........................................
........................................
   ——
   10
```

```
........................................
........................................
........................................
........................................
........................................
   ——
   10
```

```
........................................
........................................
........................................
........................................
........................................
   ——
   10
```

```
........................................
........................................
........................................
........................................
........................................
   ——
   10
```

```
........................................
........................................
........................................
........................................
........................................
   ——
   10
```

yes

Do you prefer giving to receiving gifts?

no

no

Do you get bored easily?

yes

yes

Do you always finish a task before starting the next one?

no

choco chunk

You are warm, kind, and oh-so generous!

lemon cream

You are full of zest and lots of fun!

butterfly cake

You are a gentle dreamer who flits from one thing to another!

celebrity

Think of your favorite **rock groups** and **TV shows** and replace their characters or members with **you** and **your friends**

First, write the name of a show or group in one of the small boxes. Then write your names on the left-hand side and the group members' or TV characters' names on the right.

. . . . as . . . .

. . . . as . . . .

. . . . as . . . .

. . . . as . . . .

. . . . as . . . .

. . . . as . . . .

. . . . as . . . .

. . . . as . . . .

. . . . as . . . .

. . . . as . . . .

. . . . as . . . .

. . . . as . . . .

. . . . as . . . .

. . . . as . . . .

. . . . as . . . .

. . . . as . . . .

doubles

.... as ....
.... as ....
.... as ....
.... as ....
.... as ....
.... as ....
.... as ....
.... as ....

.... as ....
.... as ....
.... as ....
.... as ....
.... as ....
.... as ....
.... as ....
.... as ....

.... as .... as ....
.... as .... as ....
.... as .... as ....
.... as .... as ....
.... as .... as ....

How to draw
a perfect star

You can draw a perfect star using just 5 straight lines!
Follow these easy steps:

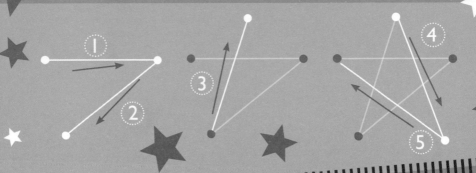

What was the longest film ever shown at the cinema?

The longest film ever was a Chinese film called **The Burning of the Red Lotus Temple**. At **27 hours**, it was so long that it was shown in **18 parts** between 1928 and 1931!

America's top 5 ice-cream flavors:

1) Vanilla
2) Chocolate
3) Neapolitan
4) Strawberry
5) Cookies and Cream

My top 5 ice-cream flavors:

1) . . . .
2) . . . .
3) . . . .
4) . . . .
5) . . . .

DID YOU KNOW? Over half of your body is made of water!

Make your own ice-cream flavor by mixing vanilla ice cream with fruit, crushed cookies, or your favorite chocolate bar chopped up into tiny pieces.

What number comes next?

5 4 10 8 15 12 20 _

Answer: The next number in the sequence is 16.

random
decision maker

Close your eyes, turn the page upside down, then swirl your finger in the air and let it land anywhere on the page. Decision made!

Try a new hairstyle.

Finish your homework.

Draw a cartoon of your favorite teacher.

Clean your room.

Think up nicknames for everyone in your family.

Search "paper folding" on You Tube and learn a new trick!

Invent a new dance.

Enter your favorite food into You Tube and see what comes up.

Take your favorite song and write new lyrics for it.

Try a book by an author you've never read before.

make mini-cards
and envelopes

Totally tiny cards to make for your best buddies!

Never put mini-cards in the mail because they are just too small!

1) Cut out a card, fold it in half, and write a tiny message inside.

2) Cut out an envelope and carefully fold it along the lines.

3) Stick the envelope together with tiny dots of glue.

Glue here!

Draw your own stamp!

Add sequins or glitter for extra sparkle. Make sure that the glue and ink is dry before you put your card in its envelope!

If you don't want to
cut up your book, trace
these templates, and
design your own cards
and envelopes.

Card template

Envelope template

99 puppy names!

Scamp	Scrap	Bounce	Bruno	Rocky	Dogger	Blackie	Buddy	Peanuts
Patch	Yo-Yo	Trouble	Towser	Bobby	Henry	Patch	Sandy	Noodles
Tom	Ross	Rusty	Minty	Guss	Doug	Rex	Scott	Flame
Bailey	Ace	Bacon	Kent	Sid	Scruff	Larry	Wilson	Admiral
Alfie	Alvin	Banjo	Jake	Kane	Levi	Apollo	Dino	Chips
Champ	Oscar	Bart	Tiger	Abby	Amy	Barbi	Apple	Lexi
Izzy	Maple	Milie	Gracie	Roxy	Kayle	Daisy	Pearl	Ali
Pippa	Jazzy	Clara	Connie	Noodle	Suzy	Pixie	Bonnie	Chloe
Ebony	Tess	Goldie	Fern	April	Eddie	Ella	Penny	Peaches
Coco	Asha	Pip	Biba	Mandy	Tulip	Petal	Coffee	Mindy
Bella	Brandi	Star	Pink	Stella	Lucy	Lara	Lady	Molly

always forgetting **where** you put your phone?

Keep it safe in the easiest-to-make phone stand **ever!**

1 Take the plastic lid from an empty jar. The lid needs to be about 2 ½ in (6.5 cm) in diameter and 1 in (2.5 cm) deep.

2 Decorate the outside edge with stickers, or if you're feeling creative, carefully glue a piece of ribbon around the lid and decorate it with sequins.

3 Place the holder on your desk, by your bed, or on a shelf – ready for when you finish your call!

FANTASY SLEEPOVER

If you could invite 5 famous guests who would they be?

Q Who holds the record for the longest hair in the world?

A Xie Qiuping from China began to grow her hair in 1973. Thirty years later, her hair had grown to over 18 ft (5.6 m)!

rearrange

the random letters to reveal 4 things you'd find in a hair salon!

derry

srossics

ormirr

rellors

Answers: dryer, scissors, mirror, and rollers.

Who isn't in the Black Eyed Peas?

Fergie

Will.i.am

Taboo

Apl.de.ap

Will-u-r

Answer: Will-u-r

longest

hair &
make-up
studio

Give the models a whole new look

with fierce make-up shades and hair highlights.

keep ♥ trade

Look at the list below, and then decide what you'd keep, what you'd swap for something else, and what you'd throw away!

1   DVD player   MP3   Watch

2   Vase of flowers   Bowl of apples   Plate of cookies

3   Black nail polish   Green eye shadow   Orange lipstick

4   Minnie Mouse T-shirt   *Spongebob* T-shirt   Jonas T-shirt

5   French fries   Broccoli   Chocolate shake

6   Books: *How to draw*   *How to knit*   *How to bake*

7   Biker jacket   Skinny jeans   Converse trainers

or **trash**?

8   Mini fridge   TV   Hair crimper

9   *Gossip Girl* DVD   Bow Tie Alice band   4GB Memory stick

10   Bowling shoes   Ski boots   Swimming goggles

11   Bowl of chips   Bowl of popcorn   Bowl of oatmeal

12   Black leggings   Silver leggings   Purple ankle boots

13   Recorder   Guitar   Tambourine

14   Perfume by: Avril Lavigne   Britney Spears   Victoria Beckham

15   Checked shirt   Floral Skirt   Fluorescent bangles

16   Autographs: Vanessa Hudgens   Simon Cowell   Michelle Obama

random puzzles

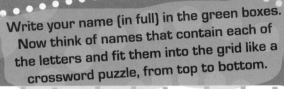

Write your name (in full) in the green boxes. Now think of names that contain each of the letters and fit them into the grid like a crossword puzzle, from top to bottom.

Which number doesn't belong

90 63 15 81 30 72 9 42

48 96 21 57 36 54 66 87 12

28 24 99 18 33 6 84 27

There are three items of clothing mixed up in this sequence. All the letters are in the correct order – figure out which one is missing.

D S S R K H E _ O S R E S T S

GIRLS' NAMES

BOYS' NAMES

Write 6 girls' names in the left column and six boys' names in the right column. The first letter of the boys' names must be the last letter of the girls' names.

designer

Design your own shoe collection

doodle shoes

Add heels, buckles, laces, straps, and patterns to create your own collection of designer shoes.

Random shoe facts

Until 1818, there was no such thing as a right shoe and a left shoe – the same shape had to be squeezed onto each foot!

The 14th century saw one of the first shoe fashions – long pointy ends that could be as long as the shoe itself!

In 2004, supermodel Naomi Campbell caused a sensation when she fell off her 9 in (23 cm) platform shoes while strutting on the catwalk!

Write your autobiography

Do you have a story that needs to be told?
Then write your autobiography – the story of your fabulous life!
Before you start, spend some time thinking about the important
things you want to write about and then plan your chapters.

Here's an easy way to get going . . .

1 Write a column of
numbers from zero
to your current age.
Write the year you
were born next to
"0" and then all the
following years up
until this year.

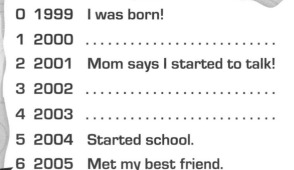

0	1999	I was born!
1	2000	. . . .
2	2001	Mom says I started to talk!
3	2002	. . . .
4	2003	. . . .
5	2004	Started school.
6	2005	Met my best friend.
7	2006	My first lead in a school play.
8	2007	Best vacation ever!
9	2008	Fell off my bike and broke my leg.
10	2009	. . . .

2 Think of the most interesting or important things that have happened
in your life, for example, your first day at school, your most amazing
vacation, or when you met your best friend. Then list these events next
to the year they happened. Some events will have occurred when you
were very young, so ask your mom if you can't really remember them.

3 Next give each event a title, for example, "The day I met my best friend." Each of these titles will be your chapter headings. Here are some things to think about when you are planning each chapter:

When it happened
This doesn't have to be an exact date; it can be the first day of school, a hot, sunny day, or a special day like Christmas or your birthday.

Where it happened
Try to remember everything from the exact location to the weather.

The day I met my best friend!

Time: ....

Place: ....

People: ....

How I felt: ....

Who else was there?
Were they friends, relatives or strangers? What were their names and what did they look like?

How I felt – this part is very important.
How were you feeling that day – happy, sad, bored, excited? How did the important event make you feel?

4 Now that you have a plan for your story, you are ready to write! Write as much or as little as you like – make some of it rhyme or add illustrations if you want. At the end of your story, write down your dreams for the future. Find a beautiful book to record your story, and you'll have a keepsake to treasure forever!

Which is the BIGGEST ?

Put these countries in size order – biggest first!

France

Great Britain

Australia

United States of America

Russia

WHICH OF THESE CELEBS HAS NOT STARRED IN A TV SHOW?

Janet Jackson

Rihanna

Will Smith

Vanessa Hudgens

Justin Timberlake

Randomize your laces!

Snaz up your sneakers with new-look laces. Take out your laces, then rethread them into your sneakers, adding different colored **beads** as you loop through the holes. For extra randomness, use **different colored** laces.

Stare at this picture for 30 seconds.

Now cover it up and draw a line through the 5 objects that were NOT in the box.

random recall

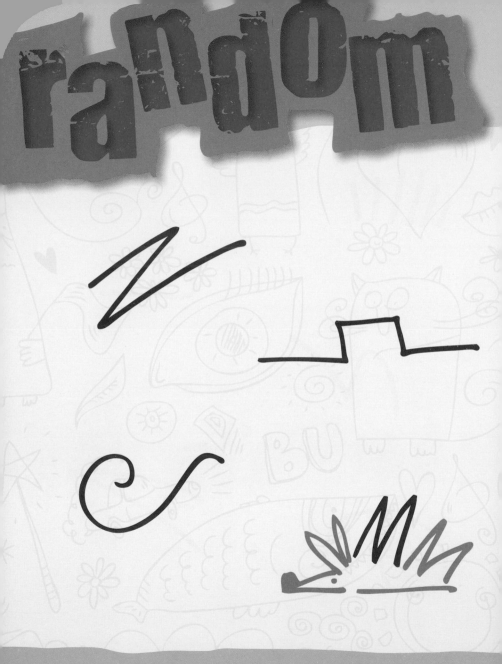

random

Transform these doodles into works of art by

adding arms, legs, faces, or anything you want!

RANDOM LIST NO. 3

What's the most random ...

1. pizza topping you've ever seen?

2. pizza topping you've ever eaten?

3. item under your bed?

10. color you've ever painted your fingernails?

11. teacher in your school?

12. member of your family?

13. game you've ever played?

14. item in your school bag?

15. competition you've ever entered?

4. celebrity on the planet?

5. day of the week?

6. hair color you've ever seen?

7. store in your town?

8. pet name you've ever heard?

9. pet you've ever had?

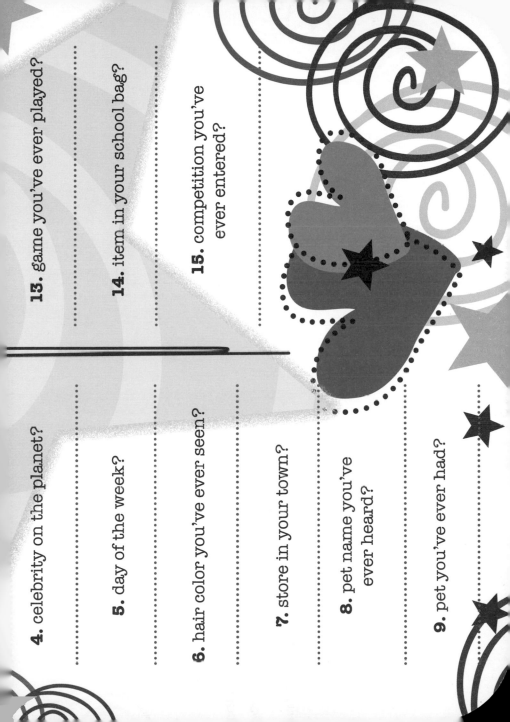

totally random

Can you make a single sentence from a random list of six words?

You need two dice and a watch to time yourselves. Throw the dice to pick a word from each category. Write the words on a piece of paper. You now have up to 30 seconds to use all the words in one sentence – it can be totally random but it must make sense! Score 10 points if you say your sentence in 15 seconds or less, 5 points if you say it in 15–20 seconds, and 1 point if you say it in 20–30 seconds.

PEOPLE

2   Rock star

3   Princess

4   TV host

5   Millionaire

6   Fashion designer

7   Doctor

8   Astronaut

9   Dancer

10   Prince

11   Fashion model

12   Football player

NAMES

2   Herbert

3   Augustus

4   Cordelia

5   Clifford

6   Ethel

7   Myrtle

8   Percival

9   Albert

10   Gwendolyn

11   Prudence

12   Enid

LOCATION

2 Moon
3 London
4 New York
5 Australia
6 Jungle
7 Desert
8 Ocean
9 Supermarket
10 Theater
11 TV studio
12 Mountain top

RANDOM WORD

2 Amazing
3 Incredible
4 Gross
5 Smelly
6 Enormous
7 Fabulous
0 Unbelievable
9 Tiny
10 Beautiful
11 Awesome
12 Crazy

OBJECT

2 Cell phone
3 TV
4 Car
5 Hockey stick
6 Bracelet
7 Fingernail
8 Tutu
9 Inflatable bed
10 Bicycle
11 Bath
12 Socks

EMOTION

2 Sad
3 Excited
4 Bored
5 Worried
6 Nervous
7 Surprised
8 Happy
9 Curious
10 Envious
11 Angry
12 Amazed

13. thing in your room?

....

14. dance you've ever seen?

....

15. thing you've ever seen a pet wearing?

....

4. TV show you've ever watched?

....

5. nickname you've ever been given?

....

6. place you've ever fallen asleep?

....

7. ice-cream flavor you've ever eaten?

....

8. song you've ever heard?

....

9. clothes combination you've ever seen?

....

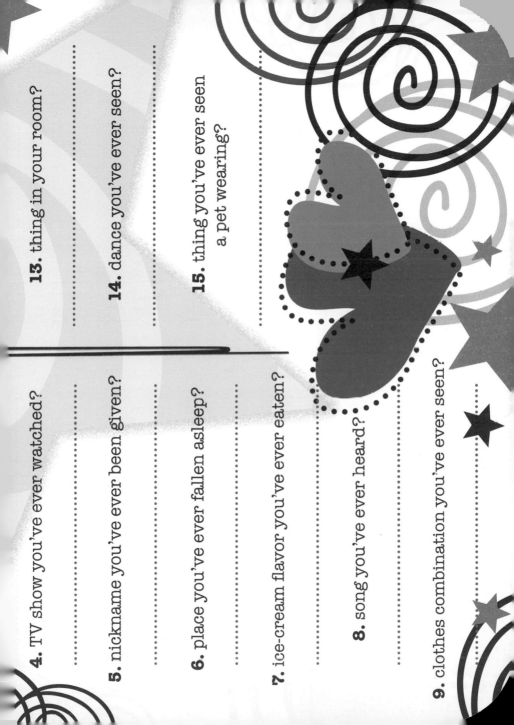

HOW OLD?

Put the celebs in age order – oldest first!

(answers at the bottom)

Ashley Tisdale
Heidi Klum
Madonna
Zac Efron
Angelina Jolie
Pink

How many in the group?

Jonas Brothers

Cheetah Girls

KSM

Black Eyed Peas

Boyz II Men

Q Who invented false eyelashes?

A Film director D. W. Griffith in 1916. He wanted his star, Seena Owen, to have super-long lashes, so made some out of hair clipped from a wig!

WHO'S THE OLDEST?
Madonna (born 1958)
Heidi Klum (1973)
Angelina Jolie (1975)
Pink (1979)
Ashley Tisdale (1985)
Zac Efron (1987)

HOW MANY?
Jonas Brothers: 3
Cheetah Girls: 4
KSM: 5
Black Eyed Peas: 4
Boyz II Men: 3